Cheetahs

By Cyndy Unwin

Children's Press®

An Imprint of Scholastic Inc.

Content Consultant
Suzi Rapp
Vice President Animal Programs
Columbus Zoo and Aquarium

Library of Congress Cataloging-in-Publication Data
Names: Unwin, Cyndy, author.
Title: Cheetahs/by Cyndy Unwin.
Description: New York, NY: Children's Press, an imprint of Scholastic Inc., [2019] |
Series: Nature's children | Includes index.
Identifiers: LCCN 2018023397| ISBN 9780531127155 (library binding) | ISBN 9780531134276 (paperback)
Subjects: LCSH: Cheetah—Juvenile literature.
Classification: LCC QL737.C23 U59 2019 | DDC 599.75/9—dc23

Design by Anna Tunick Tabachnik

Creative Direction: Judith E. Christ for Scholastic Inc.

Produced by Spooky Cheetah Press

Printed in Heshan, China 62

SCHOLASTIC, CHILDREN'S PRESS, NATURE'S CHILDREN™, and associated logos
are trademarks and/or registered trademarks of Scholastic Inc.

1 2 3 4 5 6 7 8 9 10 R 28 27 26 25 24 23 22 21 20 19

Scholastic Inc., 557 Broadway, New York, NY 10012.

Photographs ©: cover: Suzi Eszterhas/Minden Pictures; 1: zokru/iStockphoto; 4 leaf silo and throughout
stockgraphicdesigns.com; 4 top: Jim McMahon/Mapman ®; 5 child silo: All-Silhouettes.com; 5 bottom:
Kandfoto/iStockphoto; 5 cheetah silo: Martinus Sumbaji/Dreamstime; 6 cheetah silo and throughout: Taras
Adamovych/Dreamstime; 7: Anup Shah/Minden Pictures; 8: Gerald Cubitt/Biosphoto/Minden Pictures;
11: Michel & Christine Denis-Huot/Biosphoto; 12: Jose Antonio García/Dreamstime; 15: GlobalP/iStockphoto;
17 top left: rucasrucas/Shutterstock; 17 top right: EcoPic/iStockphoto; 17 bottom left: ManoAfrica/iStockphoto;
17 bottom right: Russell Burden/Getty Images; 18: Tina Malfilatre/Biosphoto; 21: Anup Shah/NPL/Minden Pictures;
22: Michel & Christine Denis-Huot/Biosphoto; 25: Suzi Eszterhas/Minden Pictures; 26: Michel & Christine
Denis-Huot/Biosphoto; 29: FLPA/Elliott Neep/age fotostock; 30: Michel & Christine Denis-Huot/Biosphoto;
33: Woravit Vijitpanya/Dreamstime; 34: Juan-Carlos Muñoz/Biosphoto; 37: India: The Emperor Akbar Hunting
with Cheetahs, c. 1600/Pictures from History/Bridgeman Images; 38: Fritz Polking/FLPA/Minden Pictures;
41: Andrew Harrington/NPL/Minden Pictures; 42 left: Oksana Kuzmina/Shutterstock; 42 right: Anankkml/Dreamstime;
43 bottom: Eric Isselee/Shutterstock; 43 top left: GlobalP/iStockphoto; 43 top right: Popova Valeriya/Shutterstock.

◀ Cover image shows
a mother cheetah with
her cubs.

Table of Contents

Fact File: Cheetahs

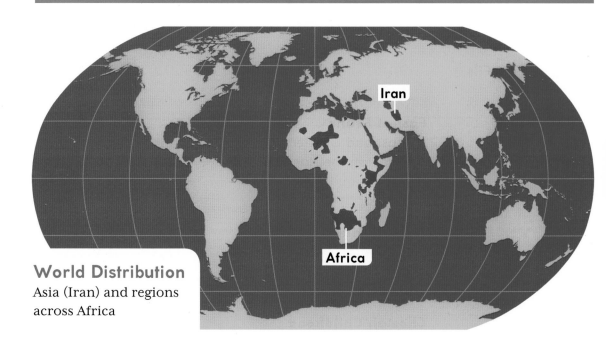

Iran

Africa

World Distribution
Asia (Iran) and regions
across Africa

Habitat
Savannah
grasslands, dry
forests, semi-desert
and desert areas

Habits
During the day,
travel far and wide
in search of prey;
use their speed and
stealth to survive;
males live in
groups; females
without cubs
live alone

Diet
Mainly small
antelope like
gazelles; also
rabbits, birds,
and warthogs

Distinctive Features
Covered with black
spots on body
and "tear" streaks
on face

Fast Fact
Cheetah world
distribution is less
than 10% of what
it used to be.

Average Size

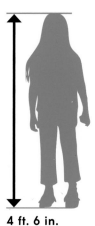

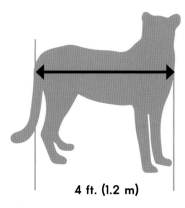

4 ft. 6 in. (1.4 m)

4 ft. (1.2 m)

Human (age 10)

Cheetah (adult)

Classification

CLASS
Mammalia
(mammals)

ORDER
Carnivora
(carnivores)

FAMILY
Felidae
(cats)

GENUS
Acinonyx
(cats with semi-retractable claws)

SPECIES
Acinonyx jubatus
(cheetah)

◀ A cheetah often gets airborne as it runs.

CHAPTER 1

Fastest Feline

It is quiet on the African grasslands.

The hot sun beats down. The impala twitch their tails, swatting away flies as they graze. They don't notice the slight movement in the long grass a few dozen yards away. Suddenly, a spotted cat bursts through, racing toward the impala at top speed. It's a mother cheetah, and she is hungry and determined. The impala scatter, trying to get away. They are speedy, but the cheetah is speedier. One of those impala will be breakfast for her and her cubs today.

Did you know cheetahs are the fastest land **mammals** on Earth? In just three strides and three seconds, these cats can reach speeds up to 60 miles (96.6 kilometers) per hour! This **acceleration** rate is faster than any car— and it plays an important role in helping these hunting cats capture their **prey**.

▶ A cheetah catches impala by tripping them from behind.

Fast Fact
Cars are the
number two killer
of Asiatic cheetahs,
after hunters.

Grassland Dwellers

Thousands of years ago, cheetahs roamed all over Earth.
They lived in many different habitats, including some
areas in what is now the United States. These cats can live
in semi-desert areas, dry forests, thick scrub, and deserts
such as the Sahara. Today, however, most wild cheetahs
live in the flat grasslands of sub-Saharan Africa, in the
southern and eastern parts of the continent.

There are five subspecies of living cheetahs. They
all live in different geographic areas. The Asiatic cheetah,
for example, lives in the dry mountains and plains of
Iran. There are fewer than 50 of these animals left.
The king cheetah, which lives in southern Africa, is the
only type of cheetah that looks different from the others.
It has blotches instead of spots!

◀ King cheetahs'
spots run together
to form unique
blotches.

Home on the Range

The area where a cheetah lives and wanders is called its range. Both male and female cheetahs follow their prey as it **migrates**, so their range can be very large. Male cheetahs usually live in coalitions. These are small groups of brothers or other close relatives that stay together for life. Males—whether alone or as part of a coalition—have distinct **territories** that they defend. They mark their territory by spraying urine on trees and rocks. Still, they risk being driven out by stronger coalitions.

Female cheetahs are **solitary** except for when they are **mating** or raising cubs. Females have even larger ranges than males. They may roam across an area up to 1,158 square miles (3,000 square kilometers). Unlike males, females do not defend a territory. So a female cheetah's range can overlap with those of other females.

Cheetahs are active during the day and sleep at night. When they're not hunting, they like to groom themselves. Males and mothers with cubs lick each other, too. Cheetahs also enjoy rolling in dust baths. When it's hot, cheetahs rest in the shade.

▶ A mother cheetah uses her tongue to bathe her cubs.

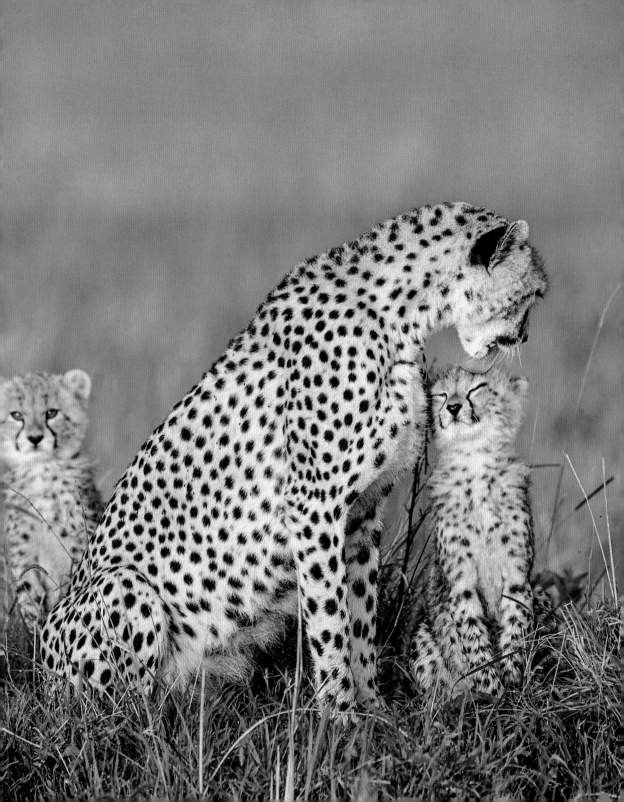

Fast Fact
Individual cheetahs
can be identified by
their spot patterns.

The Spotted One

The cheetah's name comes from the Hindi language in India. *Chita* means "spotted one." This name fits cheetahs well—their coats have about 2,000 round or oval black spots. These spots and the tan fur underneath provide camouflage while cheetahs stalk their prey and hide from predators.

Cheetahs are carnivorous hunters and live among big cats like lions and leopards. Cheetahs are sometimes called the smallest of the big cats, but they are not officially part of this group. The true big cats are larger than cheetahs. For example, the smallest adult lion weighs around 150 pounds (68 kilograms), but the largest cheetah only weighs about 143 lb. (64.9 kg). Big cats also have more strength in their teeth and jaws than cheetahs do.

◀ This cheetah blends
in perfectly with the
tall golden grasses in
its habitat.

Built for Speed

Cheetahs don't have the strength of the true big cats, but they do have a superpower—their speed! This sets cheetahs apart from all other land mammals and has helped them survive for millions of years.

It's estimated that cheetahs can achieve top speeds of 75 mph (120.7 km/h). How do they do this? Cheetahs have the longest and most flexible spine of any cat. While running, the cheetah bunches its feet underneath its curved spine. Then it lengthens its spine into a lunge, pushing off with its powerful hind legs. This unique running style helps cheetahs cover up to 23 feet (7 meters) in one stride! Cheetahs also have swiveling hips and flexible shoulder blades. These help the fast cat change direction easily while running at full speed.

Cheetahs are amazing runners for other reasons, too. They have small, light heads and flat ribs, which improve their aerodynamics as they run. And the cheetah's semi-retractable claws act like cleats to provide traction.

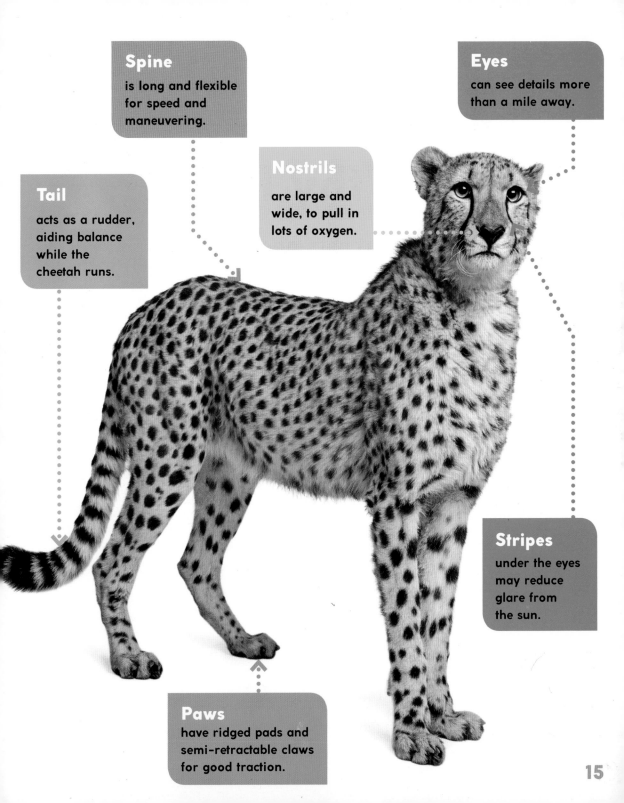

Spine
is long and flexible for speed and maneuvering.

Eyes
can see details more than a mile away.

Nostrils
are large and wide, to pull in lots of oxygen.

Tail
acts as a rudder, aiding balance while the cheetah runs.

Stripes
under the eyes may reduce glare from the sun.

Paws
have ridged pads and semi-retractable claws for good traction.

15

CHAPTER 2

Stealthy Hunter

These spotted cats need to be fast—

because the animals they hunt are, too! A cheetah's most common prey is the gazelle. This little antelope can reach speeds of up to 60 mph (96.6 km/h). Cheetahs also hunt warthogs, wildebeest calves, hares, rabbits, birds, and other antelopes such as impala.

When searching for prey in their flat, grassy habitat, cheetahs like to find a spot that will give them a good view. Cheetahs don't have long, sharp claws like other cats, though, so they are clumsy tree-climbers. They climb on top of termite mounds, rocks, or leaning trees instead. Once a cheetah spots its prey, it will begin stalking it, moving closer little by little. If necessary, the cheetah can "freeze" and stay perfectly still for up to half an hour while it waits to attack.

▶ Cheetahs feast on small to medium-sized prey.

Gazelle

Gazelles make up about 40 percent of a cheetah's diet.

Hare

Cheetahs kill small game like this hare by biting through their skulls.

Warthog

Warthog piglets, another type of cheetah prey, sometimes fight back!

Wildebeest

This young wildebeest calf is just the right size to become a cheetah meal.

The Chase

As soon as the cheetah decides to make its move, it explodes with speed. There are two times during each stride when all of the cheetah's feet are in the air—when its paws are bunched underneath its body, and after it pushes off and lengthens its spine. The cheetah's head stays perfectly steady while it runs, its forward-facing eyes maintaining constant focus on its target.

As soon as the herd senses the cheetah, the animals flee, zooming in different directions. The cheetah must decide in an instant which one to chase. Once it gets close enough, the cheetah trips the prey by swiping at its legs. Each of the cheetah's front legs has a curved **dewclaw** that helps it "catch" the animal's limbs. As the animal falls, the cheetah bites its throat and suffocates it.

Not every chase ends that successfully, though. In fact, only 40 to 50 percent of cheetah chases end in a kill. The cat can run at high speed for only about 30 seconds. If its prey is not caught in that time, the cheetah has to give up the chase.

◀ Males in a coalition work together to take down larger prey, like this impala.

Dinnertime

After a successful kill, the cheetah is exhausted and must rest for about 30 minutes before eating. Then it digs in with its small, sharp teeth, tearing into the flesh of its prey. The cat uses its rough tongue to scrape meat off the bones.

The cheetah is highly **vulnerable** while it rests and eats. Other predators like lions, leopards, hyenas, and jackals often steal the cheetah's kill. The cheetah is no match for these predators and will retreat rather than fight over its prize. Even vultures can pose a threat to the cheetah's meal.

Cheetahs eat as much as they can at one sitting, for an average of 4.5 lb. (2 kg) of meat per day. These cats do not need much water and can survive over a week without drinking any.

▶ **This coalition of cheetahs will eat its fill and then leave the remains of the kill behind.**

Fast Fact
Stuttering is how mother cheetahs say "stay put" or "come along" to their cubs.

Cheetah Chatter

The sounds cheetahs make are both similar to and different from other cats. Just like the pet cats you may know, cheetahs meow. They purr to show they are content. They also growl, spit, and hiss like other cats when they are defending themselves.

Cheetahs can make other sounds, too. Their high-pitched yips make them sound like dogs. Their low, short moans, called stuttering, are like a pigeon cooing. Even more unusual is the chirping sound that cheetah cubs make—which can be heard a mile away! This form of communication is often used between a mother cheetah and her cubs. Some researchers think the chirping may fool predators into thinking the sounds are coming from birds rather than cheetah cubs.

Cheetahs cannot roar like lions, tigers, and leopards— the true big cats. That's because the bones and connecting tissue in a cheetah's larynx are shaped differently.

◀ Male cheetahs defend their territory with growls and moans.

23

CHAPTER 3

Cheetah Childhood

A female cheetah is ready to mate when she is between one and two years old. This is the only time adult females and males spend time together. The pair will often groom each other and play. They do not stay together for long, though. The female separates from the male after mating and will eventually raise her cubs on her own.

The **gestation** period for cheetahs is about three months. When the mother cheetah is ready to give birth, she looks for a safe place in thick grass or in a protected rocky area. Cheetahs can give birth to up to eight cubs, but most **litters** contain about two to four. The fluffy gray cats are born with their eyes closed. When they are about 10 days old, they begin to see the world around them!

▶ **The mother cheetah moves her cub by biting it gently on the scruff of its neck.**

Young and Vulnerable

Like other mammals, the newborn cubs drink their mother's milk. This is the cubs' only food for about six to eight weeks. Because her body provides food for her cubs, the mother cheetah needs plenty to eat. She has to leave her cubs alone while she hunts. She is sometimes away for up to two days while she searches for food! In between hunts, to protect her cubs, the mother cheetah picks up each cub in her mouth and moves it, one at a time, to a new lair. She does this every few days. The cubs are still very vulnerable to attack by other predators, though—especially lions and hyenas. In fact, in some parts of Africa, 90 percent of cheetah cubs do not survive to adulthood.

Cubs have a ridge of upright silver-gray fur called a mantle on their neck, shoulders, and back. Researchers believe this ridge makes the cubs look like honey badgers, which are aggressive animals. This may prevent predators from attacking the cubs.

◀ Cheetah cubs, still sporting their mantles, are well-camouflaged as they play.

Practice Makes Perfect

When cheetah cubs are about two months old, they begin eating small amounts of their mother's kill. Soon after that, the cubs will join their mother when she hunts. The female's long tail may be a signal to her cubs as they follow her through the tall grass. The cubs play fight with each other and their mother to learn hunting behavior. They will even jump on their mother and seize her neck with their teeth in mock attacks. In order to teach her cubs, the mother cheetah will sometimes catch a small prey (like a baby gazelle) and release it while still alive for her cubs to practice on.

Cheetah cubs continue to be vulnerable to attack from other predators. If food is scarce, the cubs will fight each other for bigger shares of their mother's kill. The strongest cubs eat the most, so they are more likely to survive.

▶ A young cub practices hunting skills—one day he will capture prey instead of his mother!

Fast Fact
Single males
that do not join
a coalition rarely
survive for long.

All Grown Up

Cubs live with their mother for up to two years, and then she leaves them to fend for themselves. The cubs' mantles have been shrinking for several months, but are still visible. The litter will stay together for a few more months. Eventually the females will break away from their brothers to lead their solitary lives.

The brothers stick together and will typically form a new coalition. They then try to establish a territory of their own. Sometimes, they will join with another small group of males. As young coalitions try to find their own territory, they may fight with other coalitions.

The cubs now begin their adult lives. The females may live up to 14 years in the wild. Male cheetahs will live for about 10 years.

◀ Male coalitions like this one may stay together for life.

CHAPTER 4

Ancient Survivors

Cheetahs have roamed the earth

since prehistoric times. They **evolved** into a separate cat genus and species about 5.5 million years ago. Cheetahs' genus name, *Acinonyx*, means "no move claw" in Greek. Since no other cats have semi-retractable claws like theirs, cheetahs are the only species listed in their genus. Their species name, *jubatus*, means "maned" in Latin. This may refer to young cheetahs' mantle.

Cheetah **fossils** dating back more than 20,000 years have been found in Wyoming, Nevada, and Texas. That's why scientists think that today's cheetahs descended from Western Hemisphere cats such as the American puma. So how come most cheetahs now live in Africa? The theory is that cheetahs may have traveled to Europe, Asia, and Africa via the Bering Strait. The Bering Strait is a waterway now, but long ago, it was a land bridge that connected Alaska, in North America, and Siberia, in Asia.

▶ **Researchers believe prehistoric cheetah skeletons looked like this.**

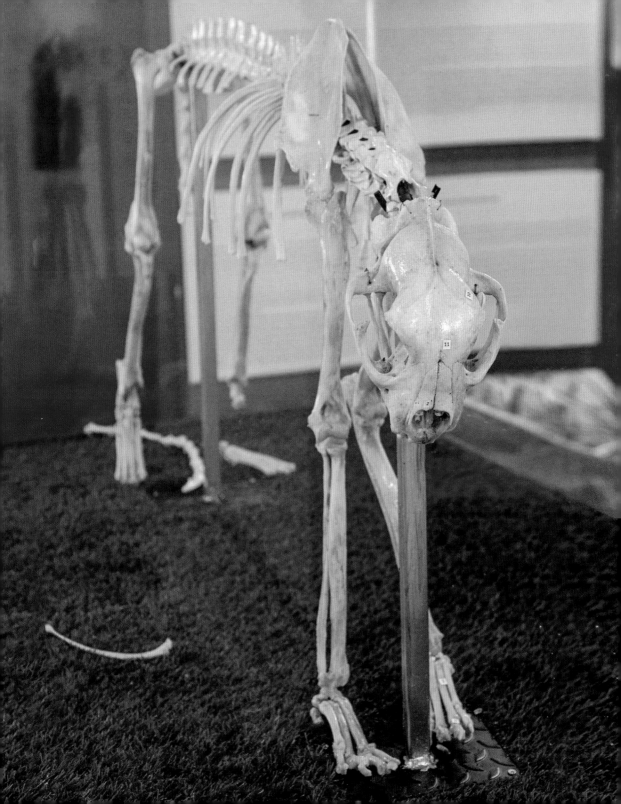

Close Cousins

There are more than 40 different types of cats (including domestic cats). The cheetah's closest relatives are the puma and the jaguarundi.

The puma, North America's largest wild cat, is sometimes called a mountain lion, cougar, or panther. Pumas are similar to cheetahs because they have a large hunting range and will eat anything they can kill. They have great vision, and live in many different habitats. Pumas are different because they are better climbers than cheetahs and they kill with strength rather than speed.

The jaguarundi is slightly larger than a domestic cat. It is sometimes called a weasel or an otter cat. The jaguarundi is rather unusual looking. Like a cheetah, it has a long body, long tail, and flat head. But this cat has short legs. The jaguarundi lives in South and Central America and Mexico. Like the cheetah, it eats a variety of foods—even fruit! The jaguarundi's unusual calls include chattering and whistling.

◄ Pumas can leap up to 40 ft. (12.1 m) in one bound.

CHAPTER 5

Humans: Friends or Foes?

People have interacted with cheetahs for many years. Egyptian tombs show cheetahs wearing collars and leashes. In the fifth century C.E., royalty and noblemen from Europe, Russia, and China used cheetahs to hunt deer and gazelle. This was so common that a Zulu tale about it was told in Africa: A mother cheetah lost her cubs when a human stole them to hunt for him. The black lines on the mother cheetah's face were said to be the streaks of her tears. Even today, cheetahs are stolen to become pets; only one out of every six stolen cubs survives.

People have also killed cheetahs for their fur and to protect their livestock. This practice of kidnapping and killing cheetahs reduced the cheetahs' numbers drastically and continues to threaten their existence.

▶ An Indian emperor once owned 9,000 hunting cheetahs.

Can Cheetahs Be Saved?

In 1900 C.E., there were 100,000 cheetahs in the wild. As recently as 2010, their numbers were estimated at about 10,000. Today, the International Union for Conservation of Nature (IUCN) estimates there are fewer than 7,000 cheetahs left in the wild, and their numbers are still decreasing. This puts them at risk of eventually becoming **extinct**.

Wildlife **reserves** provide a protected habitat for African animals in danger of extinction. People are not allowed to hunt the animals that live there. Many cheetah predators such as lions and leopards live in these areas, though, so it is actually more challenging for cheetahs to survive there.

Most cheetahs range far away from these protected lands. In fact, in Africa, 76 percent of the area roamed by cheetahs is shared by ranchers raising cattle, sheep, and goats. This causes two problems for cheetahs. There's less natural prey in these areas. Also, ranchers kill cheetahs that might be a threat to the animals they are raising.

◀ Many cheetahs share their habitat with ranch animals like cattle and goats.

Cheetah Champions

The Cheetah Conservation Fund (CCF), founded by Laurie Marker in Namibia, Africa, is dedicated to protecting cheetahs. CCF teaches African ranchers about the importance of saving cheetahs. This organization also sells Anatolian shepherds to the ranchers. These large dogs protect livestock from predators, like lions, hyenas, and cheetahs. Because the ranchers' sheep, goats, and cattle are now safe, the ranchers no longer kill cheetahs. Dogs (and people) are helping these wild cats!

How can you help cheetahs survive? Talk to your friends and family about what you have learned. Awareness is the first step to helping! Visit and support your local zoo. Many zoos have programs to help cheetahs and other animals at risk of extinction. Raise money or donate to organizations like the Cheetah Conservation Fund.

Most important, keep learning and sharing your knowledge! It is up to all of us to help the amazing cheetah keep running into the future.

▶ Anatolian shepherd dogs guard ranch animals from predators like cheetahs.

Cheetah Family Tree

Cheetahs belong to the cat, or feline, family and evolved into their own species over five million years ago. This diagram shows how cheetahs are related to other members of the cat family. The closer together two animals are on the tree, the more similar they are.

Pumas
North American cats that are the cheetah's closest relative

Cats
our domestic pets for more than 10,000 years

Ancestor of all Cats

Note: Animal photos are not to scale.

Cheetahs
the only felines
with semi-
retractable claws

Tigers
type of big cat
that can roar
but not purr

Lions
the largest of
the big cats

Words to Know

A .... **acceleration** *(ak-SEL-uh-ray-shuhn)* getting faster and faster

aerodynamics *(air-oh-dye-NAM-iks)* designed to move through the air very easily and quickly

aggressive *(uh-GRES-iv)* pushy and always ready to attack

C .... **camouflage** *(KAM-uh-flahzh)* a way of hiding by using coloring, pattern, or shape to blend into one's surroundings

carnivorous *(kahr-NIV-ur-uhs)* an animal that eats meat

D .... **dewclaw** *(DOO-klaw)* a mammal's claw that does not reach to the ground

E .... **evolved** *(i-VAHLVD)* changed slowly and naturally over time

extinct *(ik-STINGKT)* no longer found alive

F .... **fossils** *(FAH-suhls)* bones, shells, or other traces of an animal or plant from millions of years ago, preserved as rock

G .... **gestation** *(jeh-STAY-shuhn)* the period of time a baby grows and develops in its mother's body

H .... **habitats** *(HAB-i-tats)* the places where an animal or plant is usually found

L .... **lair** *(LAIR)* a wild animal's resting place or den

larynx *(LAR-ingks)* an organ in the throat that holds the vocal cords

litters *(LIT-urz)* groups of animals born at the same time to one mother

M .... **mammals** *(MAM-uhlz)* warm-blooded animals that have hair or fur and usually give birth to live babies; female mammals produce milk to feed their young

mating *(MAY-ting)* joining together to produce babies

migrates *(MYE-grayts)* moves to another area or climate at a particular time of year

P .... **predators** *(PRED-uh-tuhrs)* animals that live by hunting other animals for food

prey *(PRAY)* an animal that is hunted by another animal for food

R .... **reserves** *(rih-ZURVZ)* protected places where hunting is not allowed and where animals can live and breed safely

S .... **semi-retractable** *(sem-ee-ree-TRAK-tuh-buhl)* to be able to partly pull back in

solitary *(SAH-li-ter-ee)* not requiring or without the companionship of others

stalk *(STAWK)* to hunt or track a person or an animal in a quiet, secret way

subspecies *(sub-SPEE-sheez)* a group of related plants or animals that is smaller than a species; a division of a species

T .... **territories** *(TER-i-tor-eez)* areas that an animal or group of animals uses and defends

V .... **vulnerable** *(VUHL-nur-uh-buhl)* open to attack

Find Out More

BOOKS

- Johns, Chris and Carney, Elizabeth. *Face to Face with Cheetahs*. Washington, D.C.: National Geographic Children's Books, 2008.
- Marsh, Laura. *Cheetahs*. Washington, D.C.: National Geographic Children's Books, 2011.
- Montgomery, Sy. *Chasing Cheetahs: The Race to Save Africa's Fastest Cats*. New York: Houghton Mifflin Harcourt, 2014.

WEB PAGES

- https://cheetah.org/about-the-cheetah/for-kids/

  Explore the kids' page of the Cheetah Conservation Fund to find cheetah facts, activities, and ideas for teachers.
- https://kids.nationalgeographic.com/animals/cheetah/#ww-wild-cats-cheetahs.jpg

  Use interactive links to learn even more about cheetahs.
- www.nationalgeographic.org/search/?q=cheetahs

  Witness cheetahs in action in these short videos.

Facts for Now

Visit this Scholastic Web site for more information on cheetahs:
www.factsfornow.scholastic.com Enter the keyword Cheetahs

Index

Index *(continued)*

About the Author

Cyndy Unwin has loved cats ever since she taught her childhood kitty how to play ping-pong. These days, Cyndy teaches reading and writes books for children of all ages. She lives in the mountains of Virginia with her husband and three cats, Max (pictured), Misty, and Roly Poly.